—✦—

"I found I could say things with color and shapes
that I couldn't say any other way—things I had
no words for."

—Georgia O'Keeffe

COME LOOK WITH ME

Discovering Women Artists for Children

Jennifer Tarr Coyne

LICKLE PUBLISHING INC

First published in 2005 by Lickle Publishing Inc

Library of Congress Control Number
2004115467

Series producer: Charles Davey
for Lickle Publishing Inc.
Text and picture selection by Jennifer Tarr Coyne,
The School at Columbia University
Editorial, Production & Design: Charles Davey LLC, Book Productions, New York

Printed in China

Contents

Preface

Why is it important to study women artists?

The answer is deceptively easy. Throughout history, women have created great art but most of this time women artists have not been recognized and their art ignored. Women who chose to express themselves through painting and other forms of art were generally either self-taught, or they learned from male relatives who were trained as artists.

Up until the last century, most women had little access to education and were expected to live out their lives within the confines of their home. As a result, the home and the activities surrounding the home are central themes in the works of female artists around the world. These artists frequently depicted scenes of women in their daily routine, as well as scenes of children at play.

In this study of women artists, children will become familiar with painters who are often forgotten in art history books because of their gender. All these works are striking images, created by women who would not let society's gender biases deter their love of art and their creativity, and who, today, can be accepted as equals.

How to use this book

COME LOOK WITH ME: Discovering Women Artists for Children is a part of a series of art appreciation books for children. This book presents an interactive way of looking at art. Each of the twelve artists in this book is represented by a full-page color plate, a short biography, and a description of the image. In addition, each piece is accompanied by a set of questions to draw children into the works and to stimulate thoughtful conversations.

There are no right or wrong answers to the questions. The text can be read aloud by an adult or paraphrased to help with the children's conversations. The book can be shared with one child or a small group of children. It is best to choose two or three works of art at a time to keep the conversation lively. When children are talking about the image, encourage them to point to specific parts of the image while they discuss it.

This book can be used at home, in school, and in museums. When possible, it is always better to see the image in real life.

SOPHIE ANDERSON. *The Children's Story Book.*
1840-1890, Oil on canvas.
Bequest of Mrs. Turton, 1892. © Birmingham Museums & Art Gallery.

How many children do you see in the painting?

What is the boy wearing on his hands?

What do you think they are reading? What do you like to read?

Which is your favorite child? Why?

Sophie Anderson (1823 – c.1898) is best known for her portraits of cheerful children in playful scenes. Anderson was born in France, but she moved to America in 1848 to escape the French Revolution. In America she taught herself to paint and found success through her realistic portraiture. She also met her husband, who was also a painter, and later moved with him to England.

Anderson liked to paint children in a world without adults. Her scenes would often be set in lush landscapes. In *The Children's Storybook*, the girls in the center are concentrating on reading, while the boy in front is laughing on his back. One of the girls holds a baby and acts like the guardian of the group. The details of the countryside and the clothing on the children are very realistic. The children are carefree and merry as the sun sets behind them.

GRANDMA MOSES. *Sugaring Off.*
Copyright © 1955 (renewed 1983) Grandma Moses Properties Co., New York

What activities do you see people doing?

What does the place where you live look like in winter? How is it different? How is it similar?

What animals do you see in the painting?

What kinds of activities do you do outside in the winter?

Ana Mary Moses (1860 – 1961) grew up on a farm in upstate New York. We call her Grandma because she didn't start painting until she was seventy-five years old. By the time she died at age 101, Grandma Moses had painted approximately 1,600 paintings, and 250 of those were painted after her hundredth birthday!

At first, people didn't pay attention to Grandma Moses's paintings. But one day a man named Louis Caldor saw some of her paintings in the window of her town drugstore, and he liked her work. Mr. Caldor wanted to exhibit Grandma Moses's paintings in a New York art show. After the show, Grandma Moses went on to become a famous artist.

Grandma Moses is a folk artist, which means she never had any formal training in art. Many of Grandma Moses's paintings are landscapes showing her favorite memories. She had ten children and often included them in her paintings. *Sugaring Off* is a painting of Grandma Moses's town in the winter. Here you can see the hard work and play that surround family activities. The canvas is colorful and lively.

FAITH RINGGOLD. *Bitter Nest Part 1: Love in the Schoolyard*.
1987, acrylic on canvas with printed, tie-died, pieced fabric border, 75½ × 92½".
© Faith Ringgold 1988. Phoenix Museum of Art.

12

Find a square shape in the painting. Find a triangular shape.

Can you locate the school in the painting?

What draws your eye to the center of the painting?

Describe the scene that is taking place.

Faith Ringgold was born in 1930 in Harlem, New York. She is an author and an artist, and is best known for her large, painted "story quilts." When Ringgold was a child, her mother, who was a fashion designer, taught her how to sew. Her great-great-great grandmother had been a slave, and she had made quilts for her masters. African-American slaves used quilts not only as blankets, but also as a way to tell stories. Some slaves even sewed maps of the Underground Railroad on their quilts to help guide their way north to freedom. Ringgold continues her family tradition of making story quilts, only instead of sewing, she creates paintings that look like quilts with decorative patchwork borders.

Bitter Nest Part 1: Love in the Schoolyard is a story about a man and a girl meeting for the first time and falling in love. This quilt is the first in a series of scenes telling the story of this couple. Here, the couple meets by chance, because the girl has dropped her bookcase. Ringgold placed the couple in the center of the painting, and the rest of the image frames them. The couple's clothes and the car in the foreground set the scene in the 1950's.

GEORGIA O'KEEFFE. *White Rose with Larkspur, No. 2.*
1927, Oil on canvas, 40 × 30". Museum of Fine Arts, Boston,
Henry H. and Zoë Oliver Sherman Fund, 1980.207.
Photograph © 2004 Museum of Fine Arts, Boston.

What colors do you see in this painting?

What shapes and images do you see in the painting?

What other types of flowers can you name?

What do these flowers smell like?

Georgia O'Keeffe (1887 – 1986) photographed and painted objects from unusual points of view. She grew up on a farm in Wisconsin where, from an early age, she was interested in nature, especially flowers. O'Keeffe would photograph details of flowers, then enlarge them and study their shapes and lines. Once she had blown them up, she would paint the images. She focused on the curves, contrasts, and forms that she saw in the flowers.

Notice how this close-up of a rose shows the essence of the flower without showing the whole thing? O'Keeffe was known for turning nature into abstract images. She once wrote: "Nobody sees a flower – really – it is so small – we haven't the time – and to see it takes time, like to have a friend takes time … So I said to myself – I'll paint what I see – what the flower is to me – but I'll paint it big. I will make even busy New Yorkers take time to see what I see of flowers."

In this painting there are two distinct flowers – one is a white rose and the other is a blue larkspur.

O'Keeffe's style is often called minimalist; it includes only a few simple forms.

O'Keeffe was married to noted photographer Alfred Stieglitz. *White Rose with Larkspur, No 2* hung in their bedroom in New Mexico for fifty-two years.

FRIDA KAHLO *Self-Portrait with Monkey.*
1938, oil on masonite, Overall 16 × 12". Albright-Knox Art Gallery,
Buffalo, New York, Bequest of A. Conger Goodyear, 1966.

If you touched the plants in the background how would they feel?

What similarities do you see between the plants and Frida Kahlo's hair?

What mood do you think the woman is in? Why?

What do you notice about Frida Kahlo's eyebrows?

Frida Kahlo (1907 – 1954) was ill during much of her life, and her suffering greatly affected and inspired her art. At the age of five, Kahlo was stricken with a disease called polio. The disease made her right leg weak, and she was bedridden for many months. Then, at the age of eighteen, Kahlo was nearly crippled in a bus accident. But Kahlo did not let these obstacles defeat her, and she went on to become one of the greatest Mexican artists of the twentieth century.

While Kahlo was confined to her bed she began to paint. Her father was an artist and a photographer, and he gave her lessons in painting. Kahlo's mother made her a special easel so that she could paint while she lay in her bed. Kahlo painted portraits of the people and things in her environment. She especially liked to paint self-portraits.

In this self-portrait, Kahlo shows herself with a monkey on her shoulder. They are standing in front of a tall lush plant. Kahlo liked to paint objects that represent her Mexican culture, especially clothing, flowers, plants, animals, and colors.

In 1929, Kahlo married the famous Mexican muralist Diego Rivera. In addition to her self-portraits, Kahlo is also known for her paintings that express her relationship with her husband.

ARTEMISIA GENTILESCHI. *Saint Cecilia.*
Galleria Nazionale dell'Umbria, Perugia, Italy.
Scala / Art Resource, NY.

Describe the scene in this painting.

What is the person in yellow holding? What else do you notice about this figure?

What kind of music do you think this girl is playing? Is it fast or slow?

What kind of music do you like to listen to?

Artemisia Gentileschi (1593-1652) was one of the first women to become a professional painter. Born in Rome, Italy, Gentileschi's father, Orazio, was a successful painter. He taught Artemisia and her sisters how to paint at a time when women were not well educated. Other than her art training, Gentileschi had little schooling. She did not learn to read and write until she was an adult.

The style in which Gentileschi paints is called Baroque. Baroque painting displays large realistic figures with dramatic contrasts of light and dark. This use of light is visible in *Saint Cecilia*. There is a strong light source in the upper right corner that illuminates the otherwise dark space. The large figures are painted with vibrant colors.

Despite her talent, little is known about Gentileschi's history. Although she has thirty-four paintings to her credit, we know almost nothing about how they were created.

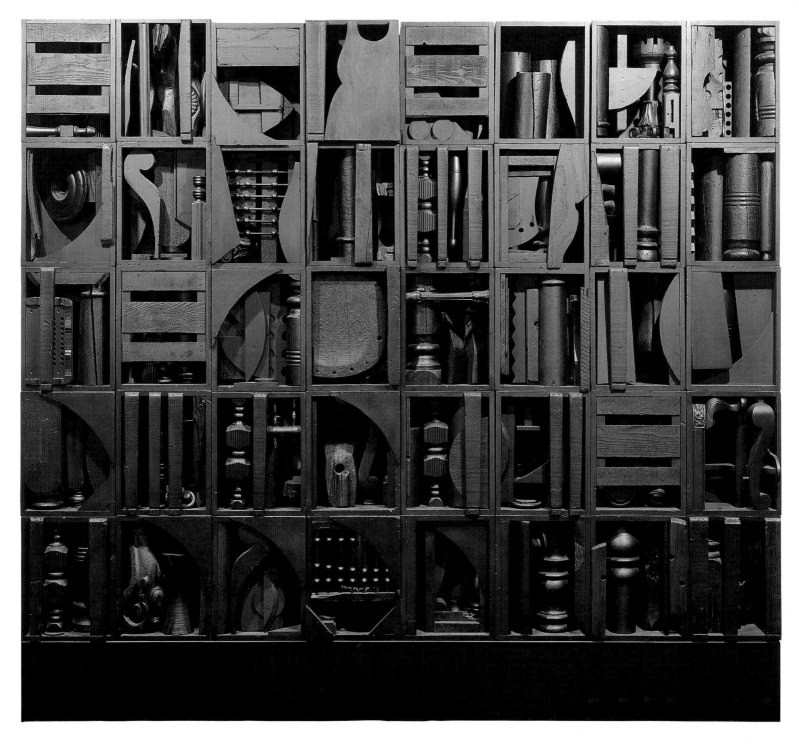

LOUISE NEVELSON. *Black Chord.*
1964, painted wood, 104½ × 117¾ × 12¼". Whitney Museum of American Art, New York.
Gift of Anne and Joel Ehrenkranz. Photography by Jerry L. Thompson.
© 2004 Estate of Louise Nevelson / Artists Rights Society (ARS), New York.

What shapes do you see in the sculpture?

Are any patterns repeated?

Imagine what some of these objects may have been before Nevelson found them. What do you think they might have been?

Does this sculpture remind you of anything you've seen before?

Louise Nevelson (1899 – 1988) is best known for her sculptures made from pieced together wood and other objects found on the streets of New York. Nevelson was a pioneer in this form of art, known as found object sculpture.

Nevelson's found object sculptures have many things in common. They are all painted in one color, usually black, white, or gold. The black sculptures imitate shadows, the white sculptures reflect the world, and the gold sculptures represent the sun, moon, and stars.

To make *Black Chord*, Nevelson assembled her found objects, and painted them black. The result is one enormous sculpture made up of many shapes and angles. The pieces fit together so well that it is hard to imagine they once existed separately!

Nevelson was born in Russia. When she was a young girl her family came to America and settled in Maine. Her father worked in a lumberyard, and so Nevelson was surrounded by the trees and pieces of wood that would later inspire her artwork.

MARY CASSATT. *The Boating Party.*
1893/1894, Oil on canvas, 35⁷⁄₁₆ × 46⅛". The Chester Dale Collection.
Image © 2004 Board of Trustees, National Gallery of Art, Washington.

Name all the different colors you see in this painting.

How can you tell the boat is moving?

Create a story about the people in this scene. Where are they going?

Have you ever been in a boat?

Although Mary Cassatt (1844 – 1926) was an American, she was a part of the French Impressionist movement. Impressionism is a style of painting that uses dots, small strokes, and pastel colors to create the "impression" of a scene on a canvas. Before Impressionism became popular, most artists created lifelike paintings with hard outlines.

Born in Pittsburgh, Pennsylvania, Cassatt always wanted to be a painter. However, society had a different understanding of the role of women in the 19th century, and becoming an artist was difficult for a woman. Cassatt worked hard and went to school at the Pennsylvania Academy of Fine Arts. In 1866 she moved to Paris, France, where she became friends with the French Impressionist painter, Edgar Degas.

Inspired by Degas, Cassatt created *The Boating Party*. In this painting, the dark figure in the foreground contrasts with both the light figures of the mother and child, and the blue background of the water.

Cassatt frequently depicted tender moments between mothers and their children. Although she loved children, Cassatt never had any of her own. She often used her sisters and their children as subjects in her paintings.

Cassatt came from a wealthy family and was able to support other artists by purchasing their paintings. She helped French Impressionism become popular in America by selling art to families she knew.

JENNIFER BARTLETT. *The Four Seasons: Winter.*
1991. Oil on canvas. 48 × 48".
© Jennifer Bartlett.

What is the first object you noticed in this scene?

How does this winter scene compare with Grandma Moses's painting of winter?
How are they different?
How are they similar?

Does this painting remind you of anything you like to do in the winter? What?

Can you find any hidden images in the painting?

Jennifer Bartlett was born in 1941 in Long Beach, California. She is an installation artist, painter, printmaker and sculptor. She received art training at the Yale School of Art and Architecture. Bartlett is known for painting representations of the environment onto a grid. She often displays several of these grids together in a series.

The Four Seasons is a series of screen prints depicting the weather, plants, and animals associated with each season. Inside each of these grids Bartlett presents items that remind her of the different times of year.

In The Four Seasons: Winter, Bartlett paints playing cards and dominoes, and she hints at other indoor games like tic-tac-toe, jacks, checkers, and finger painting. These layers of wintertime imagery are covered in white dots resembling snow. The plaid squares are a pattern of tiles found in her home, and are a recurring theme throughout The Four Seasons series and much of her other work.

SOFONISBA ANGUISSOLA. *A Game of Chess, involving the painter's three sisters and a servant.*
1555, oil on canvas, 27½ × 37". Museum Nardowe, Poznan, Poland.
Erich Lessing / Art Resource, NY.

Do you think the sisters are having a good time?

Which girl is winning the game?

How is their clothing different from the clothes that you wear?

What do their clothing and hairstyles tell you about them?

Sofonisba Anguissola (1532 – 1625) was the greatest female Italian painter of the Renaissance. She was trained as a painter at a time when most women were not educated. Anguissola studied from master artists, including Michelangelo. She painted many portraits, self-portraits, and religious scenes.

The Renaissance was a time of great change in music, literature, science, and art. It lasted from the 1300s to the 1600s, ending what was known as the Middle Ages. The Renaissance began in Italy and spread to many other countries. During the Renaissance many artists studied art from ancient Greece and Rome to find new inspiration. The word Renaissance comes from a French word meaning re-birth.

Anguissola's early works are paintings of her family at home. *A Game of Chess* shows her three sisters at a table playing chess. There is a landscape in the background that adds depth to the painting. Lucia is on the left of the painting. It is clear from her happiness that she is winning. Minerva sits on the right with her hand raised, and she seems upset about the game. The youngest sister, Europa, is delightfully sitting in the middle.

The women are wearing fancy silk dresses, decorated headbands, and white lace cuffs. On the right side of the painting a servant observes the game. We know she is a servant because of her dress and hairpiece. It is unusual for a sixteenth-century painting to include a servant. This woman must have been very important to Anguissola. Another unusual aspect of the painting is the depth of expression on the characters' faces. Paintings from this time typically do not show such emotion.

BERTHE MORISOT. *Intérieur de cottage ou L'enfant à la poupée.*
(*Interior of a cottage, or Child with her doll*). 1886, oil on canvas, 19⅞ × 24".
© Musée d'Ixelles, Brussels. Fritz Toussant Collection.

What colors do you see in the girl's dress?

Where do you think the girl is going?

How does this painting make you feel?

Compare this Impressionist painting to Mary Cassatt's Impressionist painting. What is different? What is similar?

Berthe Morisot (1841 – 1895) was a French Impressionist painter. Her grandfather was the great eighteen-century century painter Jean-Honoré Fragonard. Morisot was taught by artist Edouard Manet (who later became her brother-in-law). Manet greatly influenced Morisot's style. Like Manet and other Impressionist painters, Morisot painted with a pastel color palette. She very rarely used black. Her brightly-hued canvases are often studies of women, either outdoors or in household settings.

 Interior of a cottage shows a young girl standing in her dining room. Though she has her back to us, we can see that the girl holds a doll. Outside of the window a floral landscape sits before the ocean. The table in the front left of the painting is set for tea. Morisot's delicate brushwork and sensitive handling of textures shows a breeze sweeping through the room.

 Morisot and American artist Mary Cassatt are generally considered the most important women painters of the late 19th century.

SONIA TERK DELAUNAY. *Study for "Portugal"*.
1937, Gouache on paper. 14¼ × 37". The National Museum of Women in the Arts
Washington, D.C. Gift of Wallace and Wilhelmina Holladay.
© L & M Services B.V. Amsterdam 20041011.

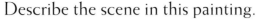

Describe the scene in this painting.

What shapes do you see repeated?

Name as many modes of transportation as you can.

What activities do you see in the streets of your own town or city?

Sonia Delaunay (1885–1979) was born in the Ukraine, a country in Eastern Europe. At the age of 19, she moved to Paris to study art, and she remained there for most of her life. Although Delaunay was primarily a painter, she often devoted her artistic skills to creating costumes and sets for Russian ballets. She also designed furniture, tapestries, textiles, and book illustrations.

In *Study for "Portugal"*, Delaunay depicts her memories of traveling through Portugal during World War I. She sketched this large mural for the Railroad Pavilion at the Paris World Fair of 1937. This fair celebrated recent advances in transportation, such as trains and airplanes. Delaunay created lively street scenes using bright patches of color to form the objects in the painting – men and women, ox-drawn carts, houses, and boats. In her mural, Delaunay painted repeating arches in the background of all four sections of the artwork. Notice how the arches get lower and lower from right to left; this is so viewers can pretend they are traveling across the scene inside their own imaginary train.

Sonia Delaunay was married to Robert Delaunay, a famous and talented painter in his own right. They inspired each other to create new styles of abstract art.

Go back and look through the paintings in this book.

Which artwork is your favorite for today? Why?

Which scene would you like to be in?

Choose an artist and make your own drawing in their style.

Return to this book another day and you may discover something new about these women artists.

Keep looking!